STAND OUT: LEADERS ARE TRENDSETTERS, NOT TREND FOLLOWERS

STAND OUT: LEADERS ARE TRENDSETTERS, NOT TREND FOLLOWERS

L. DAVID HARRIS

CONTENTS

SPECIAL THANKS & DEDICATION

Big shout to my literary alter ego, "Adam," who helps me to get some of my secular ideas into print while I continue to work hard on my spiritual books. He makes DavidWritesALot.com a more efficient machine.

I have published a novella about this mystery character appropriately titled, "Adam: My Literary Alter Ego." Get your copy today!

This book is dedicated to my good friend, Jay Moore of www.jaylivingfree.com. Always remember to set trends, don't just follow. #higherheights

PREFACE

Let's talk about a florist named George.

George became a florist when he was still in his early 20s. He taught himself the fine and beautiful art of arranging flowers.

George's reputation grew slowly; he became known for his exquisite, intricate designs to fit virtually any budget. His work was featured at large, international corporate events, political gatherings and national sporting events as well.

Over the course of 40 years, George worked for more than 15 florists in a wide area. He found that in each of his jobs, several designers eventually adopted and attempted to imitate his designs. It seemed none of them could, no matter how much they may have tried, achieve George's level of floral expertise.

George was a self-taught florist and trendsetter. The contemporaries in his industry followed his lead.

You've picked up this book because you, too, want to become a trendsetter, an industry leader; you want to stand out above the crowd and take your industry to the next level.

The question becomes "How exactly does one become a trendsetter?"

Through this book, we will explore what it means to be an industry leader and a trendsetter. From there, we will talk about various practices you can put into place right now to make sure you get the edge on your competition. Throughout the book, we will comb through the archives of industry giants and figure out what makes the men and women behind some of the most successful companies and agencies in the world and what makes them so good at what they do.

Leadership is not out of reach if you're willing to work for it. Success favors the bold, so on we go!

WHAT IS A TRENDSETTER?

A trendsetter is defined as an individual who leads the way in fashion or ideas.

Sounds easy enough, right?

Well, no, not really; that's why there are entire books written on the subject – including this one!

To be a trendsetter, one must first have a degree of popularity. You've got to be likeable, because if there's one thing that's important in the workplace as well as outside, it's knowing how to be socially acceptable.

This isn't something that necessarily comes naturally. Some of us are awkward around other people. Others of us don't necessarily have a lot of social interaction outside of a tight circle.

My friend (you might call him my literary alter ego), Adam has found himself in both situations. He still cringes a bit when he looks back on his high school days. The feelings didn't get any better when he looks back on his identity-crisis days of college. Well, even some interactions with his family nowadays make him feel a little off-kilter.

That's all right. Becoming more charismatic is something we will discuss later on in the book, and it's something that takes practice every day.

Starting anything new or improving on a particular skill is simply going to take time, so no matter what, be patient with yourself!

Secondly, you'll need confidence in yourself and your skills as a professional in order to get anyone to follow your lead. These are, again, topics we will discuss later on in the book. If you love yourself and love what you do, you'll push yourself, and when you push yourself, great things can happen.

The definition of a trendsetter is simple enough. It's
the execution of being a trendsetter that's going to
take some time and work to truly understand.

Fortunately, we can start to understand and execute
trendsetting right now!

GIVE YOURSELF
A BREAK

Don't misinterpret the name of this section; I'm not saying you should stop working. No, if you're going to be a trendsetter and a professional leader, you're going to want to work harder than anyone else.

What I mean by *Give Yourself a Break* is that you should allow yourself sufficient time to really flesh out ideas and let your creativity flow freely.

With that, we'll turn our attention to our first featured trendsetter in our Hall of Fame – innovation giant 3M.

Originally known as the Minnesota Mining and Manufacturing Company, this Twin Cities-based conglomerate has its corporate fingers in more pies than you or I could count. Just to name a few, 3M is responsible for dental products, car care products, electronic components, adhesives, and so much more. The industrial giant operates out of 65 countries and consists of a collective of 29 multinational companies.

According to Inc. writer Chris Winfield, 3M executives back in the late 1940s created a concept that we will call the 15 Percent Rule.

Back in 1948, the heads of 3M began to encourage employees to take 15 percent of their work time to work on their own projects. This can be anything from tinkering with a widget to daydreaming to sketching something out.

Taking this time to exercise creativity reaped amazing results. 3M credits the creation of Scotch Tape, Post-it Notes and Scotchguard Fabric Protector to the time spent on a project outside of normal work.

The workers' minds were free to do whatever came to them just by taking less than half the day to focus on something outside of the normal routine.

15 percent is a significant chunk of the day; I'll give you that. You might feel somewhat cynical when it comes to "wasting time" during the day. Sure, a company the size of 3M can likely afford to have their employees take 3/20ths of the day off to ponder and dream. I can't do that. I have bills to pay, you know?

You would be surprised how much time you can give yourself for creativity when you really stop to think about it.

The question now becomes "how do we fit that creative time into the day?"

You know, I'm so happy you asked! Let's talk about the Pomodoro Technique.

Francesco Cirillo pioneered the Pomodoro Technique more than 20 years ago to the delight of overworked professionals the world over. The premise of the technique is quite simple. There are four main pillars of the Technique:

1. Work *with* time, not against it.

2. Eliminate burnout.

3. Manage distractions.

4. Create a better work/life balance.

You can use the basic technique quite easily by doing the following:

1. Choose something you want to get done; it can be anything on your to-do list.

2. Work on that task for 25 minutes. Be sure to set a timer.

3. When the timer rings, write a tally mark on a piece of paper.

4. Take a five-minute break. Set the timer again. By the end of the time, you'll have completed your first Pomodoro.

5. When your five-minute break is done, repeat steps 1 through 4 three more times. After the third Pomodoro, give yourself a 15-minute break. You can find out more about the Pomodoro Technique online.

Where am I going with this? The breaks the Pomodoro Technique allow, those small breaks between each work session, allow for mental release and a nearly immediate lowering in tension and stress of the average workday.

Chris Winfield said that he likes to try to fit in 8 Pomodoros per day, and with that said, keeping track of those Pomodoros could push you to try to fit in more and more work per day. We will set that aside as an added motive for now; we're focusing on the breaks between the work periods.

If Winfield manages to squeeze in eight Pomodoros during his day, he will have put in about 200 minutes of work with 60 minutes of free time. This breaks down to 23 percent of his time devoted exclusively to not working his everyday job. Surely 15 percent doesn't seem so bad now, does it?

So, how do you stimulate creativity during that down time? There are a number of things you can do.

•Go for a walk.

•Work on a list of ideas for your personal and professional projects. Remember what happened at 3M!

•If you work from home, take a shower or take a nap.

•Get up and get something to drink.

Having that downtime due to the implementation of the Pomodoro Technique can free up a lot of time for creativity and inspiration. Keeping your nose to the grindstone constantly not only makes for a very sore face by the end of the day, but it doesn't do much for your creative side.

When you have time to be creative, you have time to work with whatever inspires you and on your own personal and professional projects. When you make time for both creativity and professional work, you can get to work on starting a brand new trend.

You might be surprised what giving yourself that room to think and be inspired can do not only for personal innovations, but also your happiness, health and workload!

3

WATCH AND LEARN

Those of you who have read my books may know of my friend and literary alter ego Adam. He's fairly quiet and likes to observe rather than be the center of attention.

He kept tabs on those he listened to; he wasn't so much spying as keeping track of the conversation. The education and the entertainment of watching and listening to conversations in his social circle is generally enough for him in most situations.

Watching what's trending is very important when it comes to becoming a trendsetter yourself.

It's a rather annoying thing to fall behind the latest crazes and trends sweeping a variety of industries. In an increasingly Internet-driven world, trends can come and go faster than any of us can keep track. It's only going to get harder from here.

Don't be discouraged, though! You can watch – and set – trends! Just bear with me as we make our way to a few simple practices you can use and observations to remember while you keep your eyes on the goings-on in your industry.

1. First of all, don't overthink it. I'm not going to sit here and pretend I'm a prophet and I'm certainly not asking you to become Moses overnight or anything like that.

Trend watching is less about being able to see into the future and more about looking around at what's happening right now.

2. Trends are more than certain aspects of fashion (though understanding trends is quite critical to the industry, based on my observations). Henry Mason of the Korea Times observed that trends "emerge

from new ways of satisfying basic needs and desires, which don't change rapidly (if at all)."

3. An important aspect of spotting trends is to know the difference between a fad and a consumer trend. Fads are franchises like Angry Birds, the Minions of Despicable Me, Gangam Style – the list goes on and on. Fads are all about popularity, and popularity shifts with the wind. It's nice for a little while, but it's not going to stick around for very long. One would be foolish to be exclusively based on an entertainment franchise.

Consumer trends are longer lasting; these trends help change consumer's lives in different ways.

4. Not all trends are created equal, and not all trends will appeal to everybody. Realize that what might appeal to you is not necessarily going to appeal to another demographic. Beauty is in the eye of the beholder.

5. Keep in mind a lot of old trends never truly die. Take vinyl records, for example. Back when I was growing up in the 80s and even well before that, vinyl records were the way to go when it came to listening to music. For a while, that went by the wayside, but I don't think it was ever entirely gone.

Tapes came and went. CDs are still around to some degree, and digital downloads are doing quite well. Then, vinyl comes back to the mainstream!

Some trends have a longer shelf life than the average entrepreneur would be led to believe. As big as online shopping is, for example, retail stores are still doing just fine!

6. Just watch, be curious. Curiosity may kill the cat, but it can make you very rich. When you see something changing in your particular industry, ask the important questions – mainly why is this particular trend changing?

You may or may not like this change, but instead of climbing on your commentary soapbox, sit on that box and just watch. Be an objective observer.

7. Look outside your industry. There are innovators in career paths other than your own who are coming up with better and more efficient ways to satisfy customers.

What could you learn from them? How could you implement their practices in your industry?

8. Take advantage of your resources. The Internet's a wonderful place to monitor trends. Check out social

media – Facebook, Twitter, Quora, Instagram and so forth – but don't stop there. Keep an eye on magazines, on retail stores, on TV...inspiration can be found anywhere!

9. Don't rush it. As we talked about, trends behave much differently than fads. Fads show up quickly like a thunderstorm in Ohio and, just like in Ohio, they can disappear just as fast as they come.

You don't necessarily have to worry quite as much when it comes to riding the waves of consumer trends. They form more slowly and therefore have a great deal more leeway than trying to latch on to a fad. Mason puts it well in his article: "Major consumer trends are about deep social and cultural changes, meaning things typically won't change tomorrow."

10. When you believe you've come across a trend – not a fad, but a genuine, honest-to-goodness trend – think about how you can apply it to your company or industry. Have some fun with it, too! It's an exciting thing to observe trends and figure out how you can use it to better serve your customers.

As you can see, by observing these trends, you can come up with new and exciting business concepts, products and innovations. By watching trends, you can create and set trends of your own!

4

BE A CUSTOMER

Nothing says "I care" quite like being empathetic to the needs of your customers and putting yourself in their shoes.

Think about it; you want someone to relate to you. You form a much closer bond with someone with whom you share common beliefs, interests and – most importantly in this case – experiences.

Think about what your customers want to see, not about what you want to see. Entrepreneur contributing writer Ann Handley remembered the day she downloaded the short-video app called Vine. The app hadn't been on the market for very long, and one of her first followers was one Sir Paul McCartney.

Yes, the Beatles Paul McCartney! When she told her family, their reaction seemed to be a very healthy portion of dull surprise.

Her teenage daughter asked who Paul McCartney was (a true crime, I know). The rest of her family had no idea what Vine was.

Handley writes, "Your perspective may be skewed if you make assumptions about customers based on your own behavior rather than that of the people you want to reach. In my case, that assumption led to some open mocking. In your case [as a trendsetter/marketer], the consequences could be far more dire."

In order to really know your customers, you will have to observe them in their natural habitat.

Imagine you're a fisherman, and you're looking for a particular kind of fish. What bait to do you use? What time do you try fishing? Where do you fish?

The customers are the trendsetter's fish. You need to know your ideal customer – where they are, where they visit online, what they read, who they hang out with, their go-to source of entertainment and information.

You can learn this through online surveys (you may wish to offer an incentive in exchange) or just by conversing with them in everyday life.

Figuring out what makes your customers tick is more about spending time with them than anything else. You can glean information from everything from the most basic small talk to getting down to brass tacks and talking shop.

Being observant and empathetic is the key to understanding your customer's needs, forming a closer bond with them as people, anticipating needs and thereby setting trends for your business.

Conversation is a powerful tool; use it well.

5

INNOVATORS, ASSEMBLE!

Even industry icons like the late Steve Jobs and Bill Gates – with their intelligence, know-how and vast resources – are nothing without their team of innovators and creators.

You're no different! Being a one-man/woman band is okay for some purposes, but when it comes to innovation, it's best to have a small creative team – a collective of brilliant minds to help carry your professional projects to the next level.

In this section, we will discuss some tips to keep in

mind when building a better think tank and spark innovation.

First, we'll construct a profile of the ideal innovation team member. An innovator is not of any particular rank in terms of the inner workings of any given company. They don't necessarily have to be a high-ranking executive; they can be salespeople, middle management, interns – anybody!

Instead of looking at rank, innovation is found in those who are well versed in the industry. An innovator has studied the industry; they know their customers. Those who are particular observant and passionate about their work make for excellent innovators.

Forbes contributor Glenn Llopis turns to our next Hall of Famer – Elon Musk – as a true example of an innovator.

"Innovation requires a certain type of person," Llopis wrote. "They are passionate explorers in pursuit of endless possibilities."

For those of you who may not know, Elon Musk is the founder of space exploration technology giant

SpaceX and electric automotive company Tesla
Motors.

Musk himself can't easily be summed up, given the
number of entrepreneurial titles he has held and
continues to hold. His name is credited behind companies such as PayPal, SolarCity, and Zip2 as well as
SpaceX and Tesla Motors.

Musk dared to venture into industries that are still
being explored. Space exploration could reshape the
way we think about life and where humans can live.
Tesla Motors and the cars therein could revolution-
ize what green energy can do.

Musk's ventures cost his companies a great deal, but
he invested some of his own wealth to keep the companies alive while pitching his grand visions and
new trends to potential investors. This helped him
and his team to keep moving.

There are two critical items to remember when it
comes to bringing together your "thinking dream
team:"

1. Have confidence. If you don't have faith in yourself, you can't very well expect to keep faith in other
people, much less your innovation team.

Every member of your innovation team has to be transparent when it comes to brainstorming ideas and creating new trends. You want a team with confidence in themselves as individuals as well as confidence in the team itself.

2. Collaboration is king. When you have faith in yourself and your team, you can strengthen that bond by working closely together in collaborative efforts.

These collaborative efforts encourage the exchange of ideas, which could lead to new ways of thinking, products and much, much more.

Gathering a team of innovators is critical when it comes to setting trends and leading industries. When minds with different observations, visions and experiences gather together for a common cause, the possibilities for innovations and trendsetting are virtually limitless.

6

WHEN TO FOLLOW

In the Bible book Ecclesiastes, it says, "To every thing there is a season and a time to every purpose under heaven."

Similarly, there is a time to set trends, and there is also a time to follow trends.

You might think that goes against everything we've been trying to establish thus far in the book. If you bear with me through this section, though, you'll soon see what I'm talking about.

While innovation often requires you to rewrite the

rulebook, reinvent the wheel and create a whole new way of thinking, there are still certain consumer trends to keep in mind in order to run your professional life at optimal efficiency and productivity.

Inc. contributor Jayson Demers points out that the use of cloud technology and data storage sites such as DropBox and Google Drive have their place in the administrative and logistical side of running a business.

Cloud tech and data storage websites are part of a consumer trend in recent years, and following trends like this – in which you and your business are the consumers – can really help make your business run more smoothly.

On the other side of the proverbial coin, following these particular trends is a way to gain insight into how a customer thinks. Going back to the example of data storage websites, think about your experience using Google Drive, DropBox and similar websites. What would you like to see happen in the future? What could be done to improve the product? How can you use that product to improve your business for your customers?

With all that said, I've listed a couple positive obser-

vations when it comes to following consumer trends
in your own professional life.

•When you understand the consumer trends across
multiple industries (especially the ones in which you
are directly and indirectly involved), you gain a better understanding of what's happening now and
what will happen in the near future.

•New trends open up improvement possibilities for
your own business, as we have pointed out before.
Upon adopting a particular trend, you will start to
see whether or not this works for the company and
what can be improved in order to help you better
serve your customers.

In short, when it comes to running the business
itself, it's helpful to consider general trends to see if
there are ways to make them compatible with your
business. However, when it comes to your company
image, marketing strategies and the concept of your
business, it's best to be a leader rather than a fol-
lower.

Follow practically and lead boldly – it's as simple as
that.

7

CREATIVITY AND SELF-DOUBT

As I briefly touched upon in the previous section, confidence in your own abilities is imperative when it comes to creativity and setting trends.

It's easy to let self-doubt take up space in your mind, living rent-free like a terrible tenant who just won't vacate the house no matter how many eviction notices you send his way.

In this section, we will deal with issues of self-doubt and learning to trust the creative person within.

If you find yourself wrestling with self-doubt:

1. Focus on the positive. When your professional or personal life (or, heaven forbid, both) isn't going the way you hoped it would and things are a bit rough, it's especially difficult but especially important to focus on the positive.

It's easy to look back on your past actions and cringe, feeling ashamed at the mistakes to which you fell prey. One little wrong event can really sour an otherwise positive experience. Don't let that negative little prima donna take you down a peg! There are so many other positive thoughts just waiting to be watched instead.

2. Keep a positivity pad. Take an ordinary pad and write a few positive things about yourself on the pad. Keep it with you, and when those negative thoughts and self-doubts start to make their way back into your mind, pull out the pad and remember that for every negative circumstance, there is at least one positive thought to counteract it.

3. Step back and breathe. Sometimes when it comes to creative efforts, you just need to step away for a moment. If you find yourself feeling especially overwhelmed, switch to something else. Go for a walk, exercise, work on something different for a while –

whatever it is you need to clear your mind and re-
gain that fresh eye for your work, do it!

4. Take care of yourself. It's vitally important for
your productivity and creativity to stay healthy. Eat
well, drink plenty of water, get enough sleep per
night...it's all stuff your mom told you about, but
they're called words of wisdom for a very good reason.

5. Stay socially connected. This can be especially difficult if you work from home and are alone for most
of the day. It's important to reach out to those loved
ones who live around you. My friend Adam continues to say that his wife is a continuing source of
support and inspiration for him, and I'm sure he's
not alone in finding support with family and close
friends. Don't shut them out, especially when you're
in a slump!

The creativity to solve your business problems and
the drive to succeed and innovate is within you; it's
just a matter of you trusting your own talent. You
can rely on external resources – like this book, for
example – for ways to start new trends in your business, examples of current trends and other various
tips. However, how to move forward with the execution of those tips, choosing what's right for you and

"rewriting" the rules to fit your professional concept as you go – that's all up to you.

Nothing kills creativity and professional drive faster than self-doubt. If you can combat and defeat self-doubt before it has a chance to take over, you're already well on your way to becoming the next big trendsetter.

8

STANDING BY YOUR IDEAS

We've by now surely established the importance of having confidence in yourself and your abilities. However, showing that confidence to other people – especially those who would work against you – can be a different matter altogether.

Dan Rockwell, self-professed "Leadership Freak," offers some especially helpful tips when it comes time to defend your ideas and stand by your innovation no matter what.

Let's say your trend-to-be has made its round among

your social and professional circles. There's some dissention among the ranks; not everyone is on board. There are a vocal few who insist that your idea is not going to work.

What do you do when your idea comes under fire? Rockwell offers some excellent observations.

1. Alliances are important. Chances are there are some ideas floating around among your professional circles and contacts that you find particularly intriguing or interesting. You may want to turn that idea into something positive for your professional life, or perhaps it might require a bit more tweaking than you really have time for right now.

Whatever the case may be, good ideas benefit greatly from moral and social support. In order to expect support for your ideas, you should, in turn, support ideas you find useful or innovative.

2. Defending your idea when it's under fire isn't as helpful as you might realize. One of the first unwritten rules of the Internet is simple yet sometimes difficult to implement: Don't feed the trolls.

For the uninitiated, a troll, in this case, refers to a prankster who performs sometimes-cruel practical jokes to generate a reaction from the victim. The best way to combat them is not to fight them at all.

In the case of defending your idea, consider the path of least resistance. You don't want to sow discord in your workplace or your social circle. That's not to say your idea is not worth defending, but the more you defend your idea, the more earnest those working against you will be to shoot it down. The cycle will continue and you will spiral into unproductivity. Your time is more important than that. Take charge and don't waste your time defending.

3. Present your innovation for what it is – it's an alternative to the current norm or established trend. Invite those around you to explore the idea rather than taking up arms against those who would shoot your idea down.

People love to complain. You love to complain, and many people I know enjoy a good venting session now and again. Sooner or later, like I said, your idea to buck the trend is bound to become a target of vitriol. Disarm rather than defend using the power of invitation.

4. When you're presented with counter-arguments, be sure to listen. There may be something of value

said during the exchange. The decision to explore an innovative way of solving a problem will involve a great many conversations, and conversations are two-way streets. "Listen if you want to be heard," as Rockwell wrote.

5. Explore the pros and cons of the status quo. Again, this is a conversation, and the idea of exploring the benefits of bucking the current trend may win over more professional allies to your side.

Your idea is going to encounter those who don't like it. The key to continuing forward is to remain diplomatic but firm in your stance. You are to respect the opposing opinion, but you would do well to stick to your guns and continue forward with your idea.

You are the trendsetter. If you don't grow a following behind your idea, and if you don't take action, who will?

9

BRAINSTORMING 101

In the last section, we talked about defending your ideas and sticking to your guns. Just as important as staying the course, building alliances and collaboration is brainstorming effectively.

Inject innovation into your business keeping in mind the following observations, courtesy of Forbes contributor PJ Chan.

1. Chan highlights the importance for invitation to innovation. As we discussed in the last chapter, the best way to win over naysayers and those who spec-

ulate against your ideas for a new trend is to invite them to have input. While not guaranteed, it's possible it could lead to productive, additionally innovative conversation.

Encourage new ideas and expansions on the trend you want to build. When your innovation team is free to exchange ideas at will, it gives them creative freedom, which we've established is important for innovation. The team members should be given time to exercise and execute their own ideas.

While you should be the leader of this trendsetter team, it's best you don't lord that authority over your members. "If people are required to ask permission for every step they take, they will stop asking permission," Chan writes.

2. Encourage the testing of ideas. Even if the ideas aren't yet complete to the satisfaction of the innovator, it's best to test it out, see what works and what doesn't and re-evaluate what needs to be done from there. Ideas are never going to be perfect, per se; at some point, they must be "perfect enough" and be tested in the workplace or in the market.

3. Failures can be just as valuable as success. Our next member of our Hall of Fame, innovator

Thomas Edison, once famously said to a reporter that he did not consider his 1,000 attempts at creating the light bulb so much as failures, but as finding out what didn't work.

Discovering what doesn't work for your business and market is just as important as knowing what could change your business for the better. Failure isn't something to be feared; it's something from which to learn.

Creating an atmosphere that doesn't fear failure eases pressure. When you are able to evaluate as a team what needs to be improved, you can create a new attempt, repeating the cycle until you "perfect" the idea.

Removing the fear of failure makes it easier and safer to innovate. I'm not saying you should be encouraged to fail willy-nilly, but rather to refine ideas presented while brainstorming with your innovation team.

4. While you should continue considering the logistics of the innovation team – time, money and other resources – you can't let that cloud your vision. Keep logistics in mind, but keep it balanced with the time

and freedom you need to fully realize the creative process.

5. Have fun with your innovation team! Chan suggests offering awards as fun incentives when executing innovative ideas. For the failure that was well on its way to work but failed due to hard luck or unfortunate circumstances, that innovator gets the Heroic Failure Award. The innovation even the wildest member of the team didn't expect to work finally pays off. Give that man or woman the Golden Goose award!

You don't necessarily have to offer these kinds of awards; the whole point is to take what you do seriously, but you should still enjoy what you do, too!

By allowing time for creativity, fostering an atmosphere that doesn't fear failure and having a little fun with the work you do, there's no telling what kind of trends you and your company could start!

10

BREAKING ORBIT

Though wrestling sports entertainment-style has waned in popularity since the 1980s and 1990s – the days of Hulk Hogan and stars of similar stature – there's still some interesting and innovative talent passing through the world of sports entertainment.

Enter Neville, The Man That Gravity Forgot. His entrance music is titled "Break Orbit." While the song itself is catchy and the phrase is just linguistically interesting, I think "break orbit" is a great mantra for innovators and trendsetters.

As a trendsetter, you want to constantly be on the lookout for your need to change.

Entrepreneur contributing writer Sherrie Campbell writes "Laziness and comfort are innovation killers." I'm inclined to agree; if you find yourself in a comfortable spot in your business, you haven't so much reached a summit as climbed up a plateau and decided to pitch a tent, set up camp and have a lovely cuppa right around tea time.

Don't get me wrong; there's something to be said about the security of reaching a plateau. It's nice; the income's coming in, the customers are happy, morale is doing just fine. Security is one feeling for which we all strive both in our personal and our professional lives, and I can't say I blame you if you want to stay right where you are.

But you don't want to do that, now, do you? That's why you picked up this book in the first place. You want to be an innovator, and an innovator does not just lay back on their laurels. They are always striving to reach a higher plane!

So how do you challenge the status quo and emerge as a trendsetter and an industry leader? It requires a bit of finesse.

Let's take a look at our next Hall of Famer, Steve Jobs. The late Jobs was in charge of Apple until close to the end of his life in 2011. He helped bring the company to a whole new level with the introduction of the iPhone, iPad, MacBook and so many more innovative Apple products.

Jobs was a manager who defied convention in several ways. He devised new and creative ways to serve the public and developed trends by going his own path.

From what I gather, Jobs was a difficult boss, though it had very little to do with the notion that he was a mean man. I never met him personally, but from what I've researched, Jobs was not inherently mean so much as socially awkward sometimes.

When it came to challenging the norms in his particular industry, Jobs was blunt. Ed Catmull was the president of Pixar (a company in which Jobs had a significant stake) and recalled having Jobs come down and speak to the director of Toy Story while the film was still in development.

At that point in his career, Jobs had developed a great deal of patience and simply walked with the director and laid out in no uncertain terms where he believed the film was going astray from the original vision. The criticism hurt, but Jobs made it clear that what he had to say was not by any means a personal attack. Fast Company executive editor Rick Tetzeli described the blunt nature of Jobs' criticism as "[able to] injure those who did not know him well, but...extremely valuable to those who did know him well."

Jobs' subtle-as-a-shotgun approach fit his particular personality, but that doesn't necessarily mean that particular aspect of his business practices should be imitated.

Being a headstrong, blunt person may not necessarily work for your personality. In fact, a more diplomatic approach tends to suit more effective leaders and trendsetters.

I'm not saying Steve Jobs was an ineffective manager by any means. I'm saying that if it's not in your personality to be blunt and particularly willful, consider gleaning other lessons from Jobs rather than his management approach, such as his motivation to "put a dent in the universe" before he passed on and his drive for perfection.

In most cases, adopting an attitude of openness and the free flow of ideas assists greatly in creating new trends.

Everything has room for expansion, and encouraging the freedom to express different ideas from different walks of life, corporate levels and backgrounds can bring in innovation that can lead to brand new trends and take your company and/or career to heights you never dreamed possible. Who knows? A more democratic approach to management and innovation can reap ideas for brand new, yet-uncharted territory for your industry, product or service.

A plateau is comfortable but ultimately quite dangerous. Encourage your team and push yourself to always be examining the status quo, seeing where you can improve and expand into uncharted territory.

Gather your picnic and leave; you have new heights to explore.

11

MAKING FAILURE WORK

We've talked about this earlier in the book, but failure deserves its own section. Failure is the stuff of nightmares for most entrepreneurs, and frankly, I don't blame you if you fear failure!

Chris Brisson, writer with Medium.com and creator of TrueRaffles.com, penned an excellent article about failure.

He harkens back to 2005, when he first launched TrueRaffles. The website acted as a hub for raffles across the United States. For example, a non-profit or religious organization could host a raffle for a car or some other big prize for a fee of $50. He spent money on a logo, creating the website, business cards and so forth until he had a typical business setup.

After four months, the website wasn't doing so well. He'd spent about $4,000 on everything altogether, and he made $400 back the first year.

After feeling he had failed, Brisson started coming up with new ideas for his site. The site he built had a great premise; now he just needed a small innovation to really bring in the customers.

Brisson penned an eBook about how to create and launch their own raffles. Within a week, he made $500 in sales!

A minor tweak, a dare to think outside of the box, made a mistake into a viable source of income for Brisson.

What points did he take away from his experience so far? Well, I'm glad you asked.

1. You can't be afraid to fail. Brisson was a wrestler in high school. He was a dominant force on the mat, losing only eight matches one year. After spending

time training in the summer, he took on wrestlers the next year, and he lost 14 matches in a row.

Did he let this stop him? Of course not! He got up and trained even harder for the next season and came away that year with the state championship under his belt.

Failure is just another step; it's not the end of the world. Don't fear it.

2. Do away with duds. Is something just not working out? That will happen from time to time when becoming an innovator. However, you can't let that get you down.

After weeks and weeks of a certain working method or product not working the way you hoped it would, it's time to consider letting it go and moving on to the next big thing.

On a similar note, Brisson notes that small niche markets may not necessarily be a good way to go when trying to set new trends. Yes, you may have a good handle on a particular small niche market when you launch your new trend, but the odds of it taking off into the mainstream aren't necessarily in your favor. If it does take off into the mainstream and it does survive past the potential "fad" syndrome (a lot of sales at first followed by a quick burnout), then consider yourself very fortunate to have found something that will relatively stand the test of time.

Consider as big of a market as you can possibly serve. This way, you have great moneymaking potential and a greater chance of starting a brand new mainstream trend.

3. Fail Fast. "Create it, launch it, learn from it and fail fast," Brisson writes.

The faster you can get yourself to the next version of your million-dollar trend-to-be, the better. Remember, that very first effort is going to be the worst, and the second version will be slightly better. The third isn't quite there yet, but the fourth is closer and so forth. Innovation is much less a destination than it is a journey.

Putting that first idea out there in the public is among the hardest hurdles you have to vault. The good news is as you continue to develop your trend and break away from the mainstream and on your own, you will find it only gets better as you learn and grow.

12

STRANGE PSYCHOLOGY

Humans are very different from their animal counterparts, but we do share at least one train in common with virtually every living thing on Earth: we react to stimuli.

More to the point, we periodically seek new stimuli. When you shift your position on the couch, you're seeking something new. When you turn the page to this e-book, you're seeking something new (namely the next page).

Often times as we go about our daily lives, we experience many of the same things over and over again. When something differs, it has a tendency to stick in our minds.

When you think weird, that's when the innovations and the brand new trends come. But why is that, and what can we do about it?

Jory Mackay of the Crew Blog wrote an excellent article on the eclectic. Psychological studies have essentially concluded that people have a tendency to remember a particular event when something out of the ordinary happens and when something strikes them as strange.

When we experience something strange or weird, our brain releases dopamine, which is responsible for remembering and processing new sensations that sparks curiosity and leads us to want to learn more. Weirdness basically makes us curious, and curiosity can be a wonderful thing!

Now this doesn't mean you should run out into the streets in a gorilla suit waving a sign to draw customers in...unless of course you work at a zoo, in which case it might be appropriate. If weird is overdone – such as having that gorilla suited sap attempt ballet to heavy metal music – then the brain of spectators won't be able to understand what's going on, and they will dismiss it as something strange rather than something intriguing enough to explore.

Being open to the strange and new is what being a trendsetter is all about. Here's how you harness your "inner weirdo" and make it work for you!

1. Be Less Task Oriented. I'll fully admit that I fall victim to procrastination just like anyone else does, although if you know me you're scratching your head since you know how incredibly productive I am. However, as we've established, taking time during the day to let your mind wander can be just what you need when it comes to creating a brand new trend. And that's exactly what I do.

Taking the time to just let your mind wander for a moment, taking a quick walk or just daydreaming can give your mind a break from the stress and help you process ideas you wouldn't otherwise realize while going about your daily routine.

2. Balance the Bizarre with the Banal. There's a short YouTube series called "Where the Heck is Matt?" Matt Harding filmed himself dancing in various locations, in front of famous landmarks and with local people from countries all over the world. He's

since completed two other videos doing the same dance in even more locations on virtually every continent.

It's not uncommon to find people goofily dancing for the camera on YouTube. What is unusual is the fact that he took it around the world – through jungles, deserts, landmarks both familiar and foreign and to the people rarely seen outside of their own country.

This particular video is strange on its face. Why would someone travel the globe to capture video clips of less than 10 seconds long of himself doing a jig-like dance that sometimes has additional participants? It's weird, wonderful and uplifting all at the same time. It's a perfect cross between strange and familiar, and that's what you want to look for when you're starting a trend; root yourself in the familiar, and then you can branch out.

I suppose I would be remiss if I didn't add the dancing genius Matt Harding to our illustrious Hall of Fame, wouldn't I?

3. Don't Be Afraid to Try. The thing is if you're going to be a trendsetter, there will be times where you will fail.

Who knows how many times it took modern-day giants like Uber and AirBNB to start up? They were all birthed from strange ideas, when you really stop to think about it, as Mackay is so helpful to point out.

AirBNB is the world's largest accommodations company at present, and yet it doesn't actually own accommodation properties. Uber is a mega-popular mode of transportation in a growing number of cities all over the world...and yet, they don't have an official fleet, and they technically don't employ any drivers.

There are strange ideas out there, and yet a number of them have worked out beautifully. Don't ever forget to give your mind a little time to wander, write those potential trendsetters down and to never be afraid to try a little craziness. You never know where that next weird thought will take you.

13

TRENDSETTING MYTHS BUSTED

There are a number of misconceptions floating around when it comes to creating new trends and breaking away from the norm to create something new.

Kristyn Corrigan, another writer with Fast Company, broke down three common myths about innovating and setting new trends that are worth mentioning and keeping in mind.

Myth 1: The customer doesn't know what they want. It's not that your customers are stupid. It's not even that they don't know what they want. They know what they need, but they're just not sure how to get it. It's understanding the needs of the customer that's going to lead to innovation.

Corrigan breaks down the tale of Henry Ford, one of the less contemporary and yet still very much relevant members of our illustrious and ever-growing Hall of Fame.

Henry Ford famously commented, "If I'd asked customers what they wanted, they'd have said 'a faster horse.'"

Your customers, be they in business-to-business interactions or directly to the John Q. Public-Consumer III, are very likely not experts in your field; that's your job. Since they lack the expertise you have, they rely on you to meet the needs your industry provides in new and creative ways.

Your customers cannot create your new product for you. Their ideas and particular complaints and wants can certainly have an impact on the direction in which your R&D efforts will go, but that's about the extent of it.

If Ford asked his customers what they wanted, they

may very well have said they wanted a faster
horse...or a double-wide horse for those extra large
loads, a miniature horse to get the young ones used
to riding before graduating them to the big leagues,
or a sporty, handsome horse to woo the ladies.

These particular wants are silly – a bit outside the
proverbial box, but silly – but they are still inside the
box that is the horse.

If Ford asked about the needs of customers, they
might be concerned about the fact that friends and
family lived in remote areas that were not always
easy to reach by horse because of time constraints,
weather and the like. They might be worried they
would have to pay for more than one load to be
transported by horse and buggy. They may be in a
hurry to visit an ailing loved one or deliver an important message, and frankly, the horse just isn't cutting
it anymore, magnificent though the animal may be.

Innovation sometimes comes down to simply asking
the right questions. Switching one little word – from
"What do you want?" to "What do you need?" can
make all the difference when gathering information
from your customers.

Myth 2: Innovation comes only from the best customers. As we've discussed in chapters throughout the book, innovation can come from anywhere. Sure, it can come from the visionary executive, but it can also come from middle management, interns, the janitor, new customers...anywhere!

It's easy as an entrepreneur to get wrapped up in wanting to please your bread-and-butter clients; the ones who are primarily responsible for helping you keep the lights on; the big accounts.

The key to innovation and expanding beyond the company's status quo is to reach out beyond your established customer base for not only information but also additional opportunities.

Think about who doesn't buy your product or service. Let's say you sell deodorant. Who wouldn't buy your product? It smells great, feels great, doesn't get on your clothes, lasts a long time...what's keeping the non-customers away?

Let's break this down into an illustration. Let's take a look at our friend Robert. Robert is a prominent salesman for Odor-B-Gone, Inc. He has an acquaintance named Tom. One day while they're waiting for their clothes at the local Laundromat, Tom and Robert strike up a conversation.

"So, Robert, what is it that you do?"

"I'm a salesman for Odor-B-Gone."

"The deodorant?"

"That's the one."

"Oh, I used to use that stuff, then my wife bought me
this stick of Ocean, My Goodness Deodorant and
I loved the smell so much that I switched over. No
offense, of course."

"None taken, Tom, old bean!"

Just in that everyday conversation, our friend Robert
gathered some invaluable marketing information.
Tom switched over to another brand of deodorant
because he found something he liked better because
of the smell.

Robert can take this information to the research and
development team, and the R&D crew can create a
new trend in masculine, fresh scents that might sway
men like Tom back to using Odor-B-Gone.

While it's important to know what your current customers want, it's equally important to understand

people who have not yet bought into your vision and their various concerns, needs and preferences.

Myth 3: Small innovations simply aren't important. Ever heard the phrase "every little bit helps?" It's true in business, too! Small investments and changes can lead to bigger and better changes in the future.

"Of course every company is looking to develop the type of product that completely rewrites the rules of the game," Corrigan writes. "But those grand slams are rare for a reason, and many industries progress by similar but no less crucial steps."

My friend Adam liked to play baseball back when he was in grade 7. He and his friends would gather in the field behind the school each afternoon for a pickup game. Though he always liked to swing for the fences, he was sometimes told that all he needed was that one base hit.

The same principle applies when it comes to setting trends. It can just be a little tweak, a minor change, adding an egg cooker to a toaster or fun designs on a Panini press, that puts you and your product above the crowd and takes you to a whole new level. I talk about this concept more in depth in my book, *That*

*Ain't Nothing New (But Does it Matter?) The Genius of
Business Ideas Rediscovered.*

Corrigan points to the story of Starwood Hotel's
Heavenly Bed, our inaugural brand to be inducted
into our trendsetter Hall of Fame. The Heavenly Bed
line of linens was a simple concept: the comfort and
luxury beyond what you would expect from an ordinary hotel bed while cutting down on laundering
time. It was through the development of Heavenly
Bed that an entirely new business was created in
which consumers could purchase the coveted linens
and make their own home bed into a sleep oasis!

In short, explore customer needs, talk to those who
are not yet your customers and don't neglect the little trends; you never know where these leads might
take you!

14

HELPFUL EVERYDAY HABITS

Now that we've neared the end of the book, it's time to take a look at some of the strategies, management styles and day-to-day habits we can add to our everyday lives to help spark innovation in ourselves.

•Steve Jobs once famously said that innovation is all about connecting the dots. Those who are considered innovators are always thinking of new ways to connect issues and problems that may not necessarily have an obvious connection. When you connect products, problems and solutions, you can help create something new and start a trend!

•Never stop asking questions. Question what you already know. Question what's established. Ask questions about subjects you have yet to understand. Knowing the answers will create new ideas in your head, and the larger your pool of ideas, by the law of averages, the more likely you are to find an idea that starts a trend.

•Keep trying new things. The Internet is a prime example of what I mean. Who knew something like goofy young men playing video games on YouTube would ever make money? But there you have it – Game Grumps, Smosh and Pewdiepie are among the most subscribed and watched shows on the Internet, and they get to do what they love (play video games and hang out with their friends) and they get paid for it. It's something that before the dawn of YouTube and even the Internet would have been laughed out of the boardroom, yet the numbers are there!

You never know what's going to catch on next, so keep at it, and one day, you will find your market.

•Make sure your heart is in your trend. My friend Adam turns out to be something of a good salesman

if his heart is behind the goods or services he's sell-
ing.

He was once licensed in insurance, and he could not
sell anything. It was pretty much a failure, and he
would tell you the same thing. Why did he fail? Why
didn't he seek to shake up the status quo or to innovate in the world of insurance?

Simple. His heart belonged somewhere else. Today,
he is a self-sufficient businessman doing what he
loves and doing it well because he loves it. He's
found his niche.

Your initial drive to innovate, among other things,
is to challenge the norm. If you are not satisfied by
the way something is in your particular industry, you
don't need permission to start looking for a way to
change. You only need the courage to stand up and
change it for the better yourself!

•Innovate something new every day. I'm not saying
you have to spend 24 hours tomorrow building the
remote control car-toaster...although that would be
an excellent way to transport breakfast just about
anywhere you'd want.

Just like anything else, setting trends and innovating take a great deal of time, practice and self-discipline.

15

JUST DO IT!

Have you ever had one of those "I wish I'd thought of that" moments?

Maybe it was when you discovered touchscreen phones. Perhaps it was the electric car. Maybe it was that one toaster that cooks eggs on the side. No matter what it is, there was an idea that you feel you could have executed, but it got away.

Let's say you have a great idea for a business. You have an idea for a new trend. There are two ways to make this happen.

The much less likely scenario to make your trend idea happen goes like this. You wake up sometime in the wee hours of the morning and you have a brilliant business idea. You wake up your husband or wife. They don't find the idea particularly good or interesting.

You find similar results when you share that idea with your friends and fellow co-workers. You continue on and on, pitching your idea until one day you strike gold.

Horatio P. Moneybags likes the cut of your jib, gives you a fat sack of money and tells you to make that idea happen. You take the money, run with the idea, become rich and famous and end up sailing into the sunset on your platinum-plated yacht.

What's more likely to happen goes a little something like this. You come up with a business idea with a brilliant idea for your business or industry. Your husband or wife, not particularly fond of being woken up in the middle of the night to listen to your innovation, tells you it's silly.

You keep moving forward with the idea anyway, building it up slowly but surely. You try, you fail, you try again and you succeed.

You build relationships with vendors, customers,

colleagues and contemporaries. These people you
interact with every day on a professional level watch
as you progress, experiencing successes and setbacks
along the way.

Eventually, one of them offers to invest in your business. Having built up your trend and your business
little by little, brick by brick, you come to a cross-
roads. Since you're starting to make money on this
growing consumer trend on which you dared to take
a chance, you can take the money in exchange for
partial ownership, or you can leave it behind and
continue on your way. Either way, you win.

What's the point in my telling you all this? Your idea
for the next trend lacks value until you implement
it. You need to take action in order to make that "I
should have thought of that" or "I should have done
that" moment turn into "I did it, and I made a boat
load of money doing it" moment.

There's a popular adage that says, "Success is 10 percent inspiration and 90 percent perspiration."

We've learned a great deal on our journey through
this book. We have learned what it means to be a
trendsetter. We discussed the importance of challenging the norm and looking for new ways to serve

your customers. We learned to look for what customers need rather than simply asking them what they want; it's knowing these needs that gives birth to consumer trends, after all!

We talked about assembling a dream team of diverse workers to form new and creative trends. We learned how to observe effectively, think like a customer and embrace the stranger side of our mind among many other useful practices.

Now that you know how to become a trendsetter and to blaze your own professional path, it's time to take that great idea you've been sitting on and put it into action.

I wish you well, dear reader. Come back to this book again if you find yourself needing additional advice or encouragement. Until that day comes, go forth and do it. As my über successful entrepreneur friend Thomas Felder always says, "GET IT DONE!" Please be sure to drop me a line and share your progress at www.DavidWritesaLot.com